FIGHTING

THE

MADNESS

Fay van Burg

BUTTERDRAGONS
PUBLISHING

Title: Fighting the Madness

Author: Fay van Burg

Copyright © 2024 Butterdragons® Publishing

All Rights Reserved

Published by Butterdragons® Publishing
https://butterdragons.com

ISBN: 9789493287693 (ebook)
ISBN: 9789493287709 (hardback)
ISBN: 9789493287716 (audio book)

Cover Design by: Dazed Designs

Audio book narrated by Martha Webb

For my therapist

Nobody knows, nobody sees
The dark inside of me
Nobody knows, nobody cares about
The tears in my eyes
The thoughts running through my mind
The pain they cause me
The hurt I feel every day
The haunting ideas in my head
The mask I wear
No one knows the meaning of
The semicolon on my wrist
I try to convince myself
That I'm a survivor
That I'm a warrior
But I can't even make myself believe
So, I hide behind a smile
And I say nothing is wrong
I say I'm okay
But really, I'm not
I am not okay
And deep down
The struggle is breaking my mind

They say family isn't always blood
But every time I find someone
Who I think will prove
That family isn't always blood
They hurt me
They let me down
They disappoint me
They wound me
So, I lose faith that true friends exist
There is no one to comfort me
There is no one to protect me
There is no one to be there for me
To save me from dark thoughts
Echoing through my mind
To save me from the loneliness
That consumes me
To save me from myself
Desperately trying to destroy myself
From all the things I do to myself
To drown the pain
To feel alive
To feel like I matter
Except, all of this is a lie
Those people do exist
I just have to find them

Screaming in my head
I just want it to stop
The noise in my head
Becomes too loud to bear
Fog clouding my thoughts
Unable to see clearly
And all I want to do is cry
Cry my problems away
My stress, my depression
Everything gone
If only it were that simple
If I could cry away my problems, I would
But I can't
Once the mind sets in that dark place
The slightest thing can set it off
It can make it worse
It can make it unbearable
Once there, I become paralysed
Unable to do anything
Except, wait for it to pass

Sometimes, all I can do is
Wait for the storm to pass
Because these winds are so strong
They keep me from moving
And no matter how I adjust my sails
The wind keeps me in place
But I won't stop trying
I know my ship and my sails
And I know that I can survive the storm

Not feeling good in my own body
Constantly feeling the urge
The urge to feel pretty
The urge to lose weight
The urge to change something
The urge to hate myself
And I want to feel pretty
I want to feel beautiful
Every day I look in the mirror
And see myself
I hate what I see
But I hate that feeling even more
So, I fight
Fight against the demons in my head
Fight against the need to be different
I don't need to be someone else
Based on a construct made by society
F*ck society
I want to be myself
I want to like what I see in the mirror
I want to love myself
And then, I can conquer the world

Cigarette smoke in my lungs
Alcohol in my blood
All to feel numb
To numb the pain
To numb the memories
To numb the thoughts
To numb the world around me
Oh, how wonderous it is
To feel nothing
To have an empty mind
All my demons forgotten

As cold as ice
As beautiful as snow
As deathly as a snake
As graceful as a cat
As threatening as a storm cloud
As calm as a river
As rare as an eclipse
As violent as a volcano
As steady as a beating heart
As warm as a campfire
As sharp as a knife
As bright as a lamp
As good as an angel
As evil as a devil
As sweet as chocolate
As sour as lemons
As light as a feather
As heavy as a rock
As protective as a mother bear
As playful as a cub
As black as night
As mysterious as the dark side of the moon
As delicate as a flower
As small as a mouse
As magical as a unicorn
As breakable as porcelain
As intriguing as a metaphor

Dying to be thin, to better fit in
Working out, day after day, after day
Never resting, never healing
Eating less, and less, and less
Ignoring the hunger more and more
Losing control when food is within reach
Only to regret it later and starve myself as
punishment
Wanting to eat but fearing weight gain
Panicking when I have no energy to train
Panicking when I eat something I am not
supposed to
Earning my food by burning the calories in
training
Dying to be thin, always hungry
Dying anyway
Wishing for these voices in my head to stop
The voices that tell me I am unworthy of food
That I need to burn all the calories I ate
That I need to train and train
Until there is nothing left

Thoughts running through my head
Like a bloody speed train
Never shutting up
Making me tired
But the train keeps raging on
And I am trying to find the brake
As my hand closes around the handle
I pull and pull and pull
But it won't budge
It refuses to be moved
And the train keeps speeding
My thoughts keep running through my head
Fast, never slowing, one after another
I must focus on my breathing
In and out, in and out
Until the train slows its movement
Until it finally stops

Caught in the hectic chaos of life
A pace so fast I can barely keep up
Thoughts running through my mind
Like a runaway train, never slowing
An endless stream of words
Unable to rest, unable to breathe
Society expects me to excel
So, I expect myself to excel
In everything I do
A million things, so little time
Every step needs to be quick
Every step needs to be precise
Why can't life slow down?
Why can't society stop pressuring?
Never sleeping, always busy
Society is breaking me
I am breaking me
As I am slowly falling apart
But so desperately hanging on, I'm wondering
Where has the time gone
When everything was simple
Times when I could sleep at night
Why can't society see?
The pace of this chaotic life
Is slowly killing me
Slowly killing us all

Writing down my speeding thoughts
So swift I'm unable to keep up
Running through my mind like a marathon
sprinter
Refusing to stop
Always on the move
If only these words in my head would quieten
Only for a moment
Perhaps then, I would finally get what I need
most
Rest, peaceful rest, quiet rest
But these constant streams of words
Overwhelming my head
Like a river, never still, always flowing
Sometimes, you can hear them
Raging and deafening, always flowing, never
quiet
Like a snowball, rolling, growing, speeding
Until it becomes an avalanche
Dangerous and unstoppable
But, I grab the lever
And the train slowly comes to a stop
Peace, at last

Trapped inside my head
Caught in my fantasy world
Escaping from reality
Coping with it
Knowing I need to stop
Start living my life
But unable to do it
Retreating inside my head
Because of sadness
Because of boredom
Because of habit
I keep returning to that world
That unreal world
That only exists inside my mind
But the creatures won't hurt me
They protect me from the darkness
From my own thoughts
They comfort me and help me
They belong to me and only me
They are always there for me
Unlike people in reality
That's why I read

Crackling energy between my fingertips
Unbridled rage, all-consuming anger
Flames in my eyes and veins
Unforgiving fire that resides in my blood
I cannot control it
I will not control it
You awoke the dragon
And now you must deal with the claws
Dormant as she might usually be
Beware when she wakes from her slumber
She will hurt you as much as you hurt her

I relapsed again today
I hurt myself again
I fell back into old habits
Habits I thought I had banished
I punched the wall
I picked up the knife
A small voice was begging
To stop, to put it down
But the demon in my mind was stronger
I needed the physical pain
To distract me from the emotional struggle
I remember a friend told me
Relapses are just pauses
On the journey to being clean
So, I paused just for today
Tomorrow, I'll try again

I see through your world
Of glitz and glam
Of money and fast cars
Of luxury and expensive restaurants
I see beneath all the make-up
And designer clothes
I see the loneliness
I see the young child
Abandoned
I see the hole in your heart
That money and success can't seem to fill
I see through your world
Of glitz and glam
I see the real you

I stopped eating today
And felt sad because of it
I stopped eating today
Because you awoke the monster
I desperately tried to kill
The monster that I had caged
But could still hear
The monster that told me I had to stop eating
That I was fat and ugly
It told me I was worthless
You broke that monster free
And I despise you for it
For you allowed the monster to rage
To murder all the progress I had made

F*cking Ana made me do it
F*cking Ana made me say no
To restaurants dinners and special occasions
To going out with friends, because what will
other people say about me
F*cking Ana made me stop eating, only to
binge later on
F*cking Ana made me do it

The lies I tell myself
I am ugly
I am fat
I am stupid
I am not good enough
I am worthless
I am unlovable
I am alone
Nobody loves me
And I am starting to believe them
But then I remind myself
It's not true
I don't need to change
And the lies start to fade
And they will continue to fade
As long as keep reminding myself

I saw a tree today
And I wanted to wrap my car around it
Like some kind of garland
On a Christmas tree
But I didn't
All it takes is one little tug on the wheel
And I'd be gone
One little swerve
And I'd be done
But I'm still here

My mind is as fragile as thin glass
About to snap like a twig
And shatter into a million pieces
Because you made me feel worthless
You made me feel like I can't do anything
right
Like I can only make mistakes
You never trusted me, but told me many lies
But I don't want to make mistakes
I want to make things right
So, I left, for the sake of myself
Before I shattered on the floor
Like a piece of fragile glass

Dear body,
I apologize for all the hardship I put your
through
I apologize for every time I starved you
Because the mirror said I was unworthy of
food
I apologise for every cut and burn I made
Because my emotions were too great of a
tsunami to handle
Will you forgive me, dear body?

One, two, three
Breathe in, breathe out
Four, five, six
Put down the knife
Seven, eight, nine
You will be okay
Ten

You awoke a monster
That I had carefully wrapped in chains
You awoke a monster
That I had meticulously locked in a cage
You awoke a monster
That I had brutally gagged
So, it couldn't speak
And now, that monster is free
And raging beyond control and reason
Telling me I am nothing without it
That I am worthless, a failure, a burden
This monster that keeps telling me
I have to stop eating, that I am ugly
And I hate you for it

Do you ever think about how
A person you consider a friend
Does not see you that way
How does that make you feel?
Indifferent? Lonely? Hurt? Abandoned? Sad?
Or is it just another thing you expect in life
No one should get used to being a second
choice
An option to be kept around for convenience
And they only turn to you
When they need something
But they never have time for you
So, you need to consider
To no longer call that person a friend

My brain is screaming
Begging to be understood
My heart is screaming
Begging for the pain to stop
My eyes are screaming
Begging for the tears to dry
My wrists are screaming
Begging for the cutting to cease
I am screaming
Begging to be okay
I take a deep breath
And count to ten
I am not okay
But I will be

Once a year
From dusk till dawn
The dead waltz through the graveyard
Once a year
The violins sound from beyond the grave
Back and forth, back and forth
Once a year
The dead are granted one night among the
living
Watch how they sway
Back and forth, back and forth
In their shrouds
Once a year
The rooster crows
And the dead stop their macabre dance
See how they scramble and run
Back to their earthly tombs
To lie and wait for another year
For their macabre dance

I am scared to say something wrong
To hurt someone I care about
So, I rather not talk at all
I believe so strongly
That I am better off without friends
Than living in constant fear
Of hurting them
It may not be soon
But eventually
I always seem to hurt the ones I love

As I stare into a beautiful sunset on the beach
I cry
Not the tears of happiness
But tears of sadness
Tears that have no place in such serene
surrounding
Yet another fight
Yet another suffocating atmosphere
From which I had to escape
When will I run far enough?
When will I escape this toxicity?
This air I cannot breathe
This darkness constricting my growth

I punched a wall again today
I was so furious, I slammed my fist
Into the wall, before I could help myself
I went off track
I was overwhelmed with anger
But didn't want to pick up the knife
I downloaded a tracker right after
To prove to myself I can stop
To help myself stay away from self-harm
To stay on track
But emotions were overwhelming, still
So, I had another binge, another relapse
But I went to the gym right after
To prove to myself I can control it
To help myself deal with emotions differently
To stay on track

Before you judge
Stop and think
You don't know their story
You don't know why
Someone struggles with weight
You don't know
The traumas someone is struggling with
You don't know
What insecurities someone faces
Or why they stopped eating
So, before you judge
Know their story

I bend so that I don't break
But you come awfully close to snapping me
I analyse every move before I make it
And calculate how you will react
What chain reaction will be unleashed
When I play my cards wrong
And you try to convince me my jack is an ace

I learned plenty today
I learned that I can be happy
I learned that I can stand up for myself
I learned that I can achieve great things on my
own
I learned that I can make friends anywhere
But mostly, I learned that I don't need you
I just need myself
And that, is called progress
That, is called growth

I am addicted to my illness
To the voices in my head
That hurt me so much
I can turn them into art
Until the scale shifts
And the weight finally goes down
Until I get that feeling happy exhaustion
And with that, a feeling of relief

Sometimes, I wonder why I have a phone
If I don't start the conversation, nobody else
does
I get notices about the lives of others
Lives that I am not a part of
And the rest is silence
My phone remains silent throughout the day
My friends don't notice I'm quiet
That I have stopped talking
Because they are busy with their lives
And I am not their priority
While they are always on my mind
So instead of chasing ghosts
I write my thoughts on my phone
And I search for friends online
Lonely souls like me
Always support a stranger in need

I'm standing on the edge of a cliff again
Wanting to jump
But you tied a rope around my waist
You refused to let me jump
No matter how much I screamed and cried
You don't know me, or my story
But you saved my life
And I am grateful for you
You comforted me in time of need
And I don't even know you
But I know what you did for me
Thank you

I ate chocolate again
Not because I wanted the taste of it
But because I craved it
Because I craved the feeling of happiness
It feels like eating chocolate is the only way
I can experience some happiness lately
I don't know why, but I just feel empty
So, I keep eating chocolate
Just to feel something

In that moment
Cracks in my mind began to form
Until it would eventually snap
Like a brittle twig on the forest floor after a
drought
In that moment
You made it known
That I was worthless
You ruined my self confidence
You shattered any kind of belief
That I had in myself
And now I am fighting
Fighting to get out of the darkness
You pushed me in
But I will succeed some day
And from that moment
I'll never let you bring me down again

I decided to help myself
So, I went to therapy
And now my creativity is broken
It is failing me
My writing is failing me
Pen and paper are no longer my friends
And I can't help but wish
To be back at the rock bottom
Because when I was there
I could write, I could make art
But now that I am better
I struggle as a poet

My mind is darker than the night of the new
moon
There is not a star in the sky, not a single
source of light
I'm tired of swimming so I'm drowning
With no one to safe me
I'm tired yet unable to sleep
I'm alive but not living
I'm reduced to a zombie-like state
Not fully aware of what is happening around
me
Waiting to come through to the other side
To survive the cycle
And get ready for the next one whenever it
comes
I'm strong enough

All my life, I have been fighting
To be seen, to be heard
And it hurts
It makes me tired
It drains me
When people don't see my value
So, for now, I'm done fighting
Instead, I turn to myself
And now I know my worth

Every time I open my mouth
You tell me to shut up
Telling me my black is white
Telling me my up is down
So, I keep asking myself
Why do I keep letting myself go through this?
I think, I finally know the answer
I don't know when to quit
I don't know when enough is enough
And I persist
I keep giving second chances
Hoping every time, you will realise
That you hurt me
But even when I tell you
You refuse to listen
I think it's time for me to stop trying

They tell me, you don't look sick
But I am fighting a battle every day
They tell me, you don't look sick
But moving feels as if I am swimming through
thick oil
They tell me, you don't look sick
But I get headaches every day
They tell me, you don't look sick
But my heart beats out of my chest at the
slightest strain
They tell me, you don't look sick
But I feel as if I am going to faint
They tell me, you don't look sick
But my hands shake uncontrollably when I lift
the lightest of things
They tell me, you don't look sick
But I am fighting a battle every single day

To those who tried to break me
To those who told me I was fat
F*ck you for messing with my mind
F*ck you for messing with my self-esteem
F*ck you for all the stress you caused me
F*ck you, but I am fighting back
I am stronger than ever
Even with all the problems you've caused
I am dying to tell you what you did to me
How your words affected me
But I refuse to give you recognition
You are not worth the air I breathe
I release you from my mind
I leave you in the past
This is my final goodbye to you

The pain comes and goes
It ebbs and flows like the tide
Regrets wash over me
All the things I never got to say
All the things we never got to do
All the things you will miss
All the things I will miss
Your hugs, your laugh, your scent
I know that life isn't always fair
And it wasn't when it decided it was your time
to go
So, I will strive to make you proud
To live the life you wanted me to live
And I know you will be there

Don't compare your pain
To the pain of others
Your pain is yours to carry
Stop minimising by saying it wasn't that bad
Just because someone else hurts more
Your pain is valid, too
No matter the cause
What is pain for one
Might be nothing for other
But that doesn't mean you should be okay
Your pain is yours to carry

I am a husk
I am a shell
Hollow on the inside
Not a single emotion
Not a single thought
Just one breath after another
But I am not mad or numb
I just like the quiet right now
The silence, the solitude
Respite from the noise

I am being dragged back
Into the abyss
By a monster
That I want to escape from
But how can I escape
If I can't even see the monster
When it's hiding in my mind
When it occupies my every thought
I am too tired to fight it today
So, for now, I let it rage
I will fight the monster again tomorrow
I don't have to fight everyday
I'm allowed to have a break

How can I fight a monster
When the monster is me
When the monster resides in my head
When the monster is in my thoughts
And my self-destructive behaviour
Maybe it's not a monster
And instead of viewing my thoughts
My behaviour and my emotions
As monsters
I should try to see them as helpers
Because they all signify something
I just need to find out what it is
They are trying to tell me
And work through it
It might stop the monsters

When nobody believes you
Can you still believe in what you say?
When nobody believes you
Can you still defend yourself?
When nobody believes you
Are your problems real?
When nobody believes you
Will you find someone who does?
When nobody believes you
What can you do?
You fight to be heard
You find someone who believes you
Who will fight with you
And if nobody listens
You fight harder
You do whatever it takes

I made a wish list for Christmas
I wanted a good book
I wanted a healthy body
I wanted a nice perfume
I wanted a healthy body
I wanted a little dragon
I wanted a healthy body
I wanted a new sweater
I wanted a healthy body
I wanted a set of pens
I wanted a healthy body
I wanted a pretty notebook
I wanted a healthy body
And all my wishes came true, but one
And that's the only thing I really want
I want a healthy body

When friends tear you down
They aren't friends
When friends ignore your needs
And keep calling you out
Whilst you are already on the verge of tears
They aren't friends
When friends don't share with you
They aren't friends
When communication becomes one-way only
They aren't friends
When friends keep hurting you
They aren't friends
You can do better

I made a New Year's resolution
I want to exercise more
I want to love myself more
I want to read more books
I want to love myself more
I want to work on my craft
I want to love myself more
I want to learn something new
I want to love myself more
And I do, more and more each day

I feel hollow inside
It might be my medicine
It might be my state of mind
Not wanting to do anything
Just sit there and hope it will pass
I'm just an empty shell
Not being able to shed this emptiness inside
I need to wait it out
Wait until the medicine wears off
And my zombie like state disappears
And my thoughts slowly come back
And I slowly become more like myself

How do I keep hoping
After being rejected more times than I can
count
How do I go on?
How do I continue?
How can I still trust in my own self-worth
How can I learn, when nobody gives me the
opportunity
When nobody takes a chance on me
And it is becoming frustrating
It is starting to hurt me
I am starting to lose faith
In myself, in my capabilities
But at the same time
I feel the opposite
I feel indifferent
If someone doesn't see my value
That is okay
I will find someone else who does

I guess, I am upset
That I never seem to cross your mind
You never seem to invite me to join you
On your adventures
But when I invite you to mine
You instantly say yes
This friendship feels like a one-way street
And it's starting to frustrate me
I should be invited to do fun things with you
But you don't seem to think of me as important
So, I will stop including you into my life

Being left on read
Makes me feel anxious
Hearing someone use my full name
Makes me feel anxious
Stepping on the scale
Makes me feel anxious
Making a phone call
Makes me feel anxious
Meeting new people
Makes me feel anxious
So many things make me anxious
But I am working through it
Bit by bit, fear by fear

My mind is spinning fast
And I can't seem to stop it
The thoughts are never ending
But I need some peace of mind
I can't stop thinking about you
Thinking I am not good enough for you
Thinking that your love isn't real
Thinking that you stay only for convenience
But I have to know for sure
So, I pick up my phone and call you
Wondering what you'll say

I am writing letters
Addressed to the fire
And I will watch them burn
All the words
I could never say
Out of fear
Out of anger
Out of sadness…
I will watch the cream-coloured papers
Curl up, greying
Turning to ash
I will blow them into the winds
Releasing them as they scatter
And watch my words
And my thoughts
Fly away

Are you ignoring me?
Did I say something wrong?
Are you busy with work?
Or friends?
Were you just polite when you replied to me?
I am too afraid to ask you in person
Too scared of rejection
So, instead of telling you how I really feel
I'll tell you that being left on read
Gives me anxiety

I will never forgive you for what you said
When I was just a teenager
Words have power
And you spoke terrible things into existence
I blame you for the way I feel now
How dare you say such things to me?
You spoke my monster into existence
And you made it rage
So, I will never forgive you for that

When I'm feeling down
I remember
That behind the clouds
The sun always shines
And eventually
The clouds will part
The darkness will fade
And the light will shine once again

I don't know how to exist properly
I don't know how to feel
How to think
How to dress
How to talk
I only know
How to be me
But being me isn't always enough
I feel excluded wherever I go
And I only feel accepted
When I'm with the other excluded
So maybe, I am not excluded after all
Maybe I just want to be accepted
By the wrong people

Being ignored after a full day of talking
Makes me feel like I said something wrong
Makes me feel anxious
Meeting new people is scary
What if they don't like me?
It makes me feel anxious
When I get an unexpected call
That can mean bad news
And it makes me feel anxious
Unfinished arguments scare me
What if we are not okay afterwards?
So much anxiety…

If I don't start the conversation
Nobody else does
Everybody remains silent
Doing their own thing
And I feel lonely
Like no one is interested
To become my friend
I want to have a best friend
To be someone's first choice
And I want them to be mine
Best friends forever

It's not jealousy I feel
I just hate the unfairness
Anyone can do anything
If they had the resources
But I'm trying to do my best
With what I have

When you give me the silent treatment
How can I figure out what went wrong?
How can I learn to be better next time?
You are teaching me a lesson, I know
You are teaching me that love is conditional
You are teaching me to be afraid to try and fail
You are teaching me that I cease to exist when
you are angry
You are teaching me I am only worthy of
recognition
When I behave the way you want me to
So, thanks to you, I've learned a lot
I learned how anxiety feels like
I learned how emotional pain feels like
I learned I wasn't good enough
I learned to be afraid of attaching to people
But most of all
I learned how emotional abuse feels like

I numbed myself with pills
Because you caused me too much pain
You hurt me so bad
With your words full of venom
Screaming at me like possessed
My emotions are dazed
My mind too blurry to think properly
Awake enough to stay aware
Yet, I don't feel any pain
But for now, that is all I want
I don't need to think
I don't need to feel
I want to be numb
At least, until the smoke settles

When someone told me
We are so much kinder
To our friends than our inner selves
Something clicked inside my head
So, I decided to become my friend
To treat myself with kindness
Like I would my best friend

My body felt broken
I felt nauseated and tired
My body was screaming
But my mind refused
My mind screamed at me to keep going
To burn off more fat
To train more, to be thinner
And I wanted to do more
But my body wouldn't let me
And deep down
I knew I should take some rest
But my mind complained
In the end, my body won

I saw your name on the schedule
In the same shift as me
And anxiety spiked
Because what you said
Still rings through my mind
Your words hurt me
And made me question myself
I was eating myself up
Too afraid to be myself
Too afraid to let my light shine
But I am not letting you
And your stupid words
Dictate who I am anymore
I am stronger than that

When I have one of those days
When everything goes wrong
From the moment I open my eyes
Here is what I do to get through
I talk to myself with love
I wear my favourite clothes
I make myself a nice meal
And I listen to my favourite music
I take the day minute by minute
Hour by hour
I breathe in and breathe out
Knowing that tomorrow, I will be better

People expect me to be free of problems
Because I'm a psychologist
They think I'm okay
But I am not, not all the time
I have my own issues
I have my dark moments
I have my inner demons
My monsters
But they help me
By knowing that I'm not perfect
And having space for acceptance
They make me better at what I do
And aid those who need me to

What happens with me
Should be my choice
But you're not giving me one
I feel pressured by you
To do with myself as you dictate
I don't want to take the pills
They make me feel all sorts of wrong
And they don't work the way you want them to
So now I just sit here
Pills in hand
Wanting to toss them out
But forced to take them
Swallow, gulp
Gone, they are
I didn't think I would deserve this
But you got your way, this time

I am keeping myself small
Agreeing with everything you say
Because I'm too tired to fight
My pills are keeping me calm
My pills are keeping me prisoner
This isn't who I am
But I feel like you've left me no choice
So, now I live my days in a daze
Too numb to even protest
Too cloudy for my light to shine

Sledgehammer returned today
Pounding on my knees, my ankles, my hips
Anvil is weighing down my legs
Barbed wire is wrapping around my thighs
And it f*cking hurts
I am being punished for having fun
Punished violently
Nothing eases the pain
The cold no longer helping
The elevation no longer relieving
Movement, no longer easing
So, I wrestle with the sledgehammer
I grab it with my hands
I try to stop it
But it refuses to stop
So, until it stops, I keep writing

I write because it helps me process my pain
It helps me deal with sadness
It helps me when I'm angry
Writing is always there for me
Whereas people, they tend to let me down
My pens and notebooks don't judge
When I'm angry, I write
When I'm sad, I write
When I'm scared, I write
When I'm happy, I write
When I feel something worth writing
I write

I always carry a notebook and a pen
Tortured poet that I am
Tortured by my thoughts
Tortured by my feelings
They haunt me in the middle of the night
Forcing me to write them down
Get them out of my head
Lest they keep plaguing me
Little thoughts
Like earworms in my head

There is something special about
Zoos, and theme parks, and fairs
That makes me incredibly happy
It fills me with a childlike wonder
I forget all my worries
And life seems great
Maybe that's why I love them so much
Why I look forward to every visit
Because I forget everyday life
And for a moment, I am truly free

When someone tells you about
Their weight and eating problems
They hope for sympathy
A kind word, a shoulder to cry on
So, stop yourself from being mean
Don't tell them they have no willpower
Or that they should just eat less
You have no idea what they're going through
How they struggle with their monsters
That tell them to stop eating
Or purge, or eat more
They fight every day
Desperately trying not to give in
And some days, they succeed
So, if you want to help
Don't judge, just listen

When I know I am going out to eat
I skip meals to save calories
I restrict myself beforehand
But today, I made an exception
I ate breakfast and it felt good
The voices telling me to stop eating
Were finally silenced by the voices
Telling me it is better for me to eat

You decided to hurt me
Because you cannot accept
Who I am
So, I wanted to cut myself again
And watch your hurtful words
Stream out of my body
With the red of my blood
But I didn't
I refused to let your actions
Form a permanent mark
On my body
So, I put down the knife
And wrote this poem instead

I feel an aching cold in my bones
I am so tired
It cannot be fixed with blankets and hot tea
All I need is sleep
And I cannot seem to catch any
Rest seems to be avoiding me
The aching cold, the shivers
That nothing can calm
I take it as a sign from my body
And I need to listen

Sometimes, I feel emotions
So intense, so vivid
Anger, fear, hurt, sadness
So strong and so consuming
They cause me to say things
That I don't mean to say
And I hurt the ones I never meant to hurt
But when my emotions rule my brain
I cannot help it, I cannot escape it
They just spill before I can stop them
And then the shame comes
Shame for losing control
Shame for being a mess

When you spend so much time
Trying to survive
And running from the pain
Do you even remember what you were running
from?
The most likely answer is that you don't
If you spend years running
You tend to forget why
If you don't know the reason
Stop running
Stop fleeing
Breathe
Relax
Take a break
It will be okay

If you never get out of your comfort zone
If you never push yourself past your limits
If you never challenge yourself
You are never going to grow
But growth hurts, growth is painful
It is brutal and ugly
It takes time, it takes work
But don't be afraid
Growth will take you to beautiful places
Embrace it

Mascara is running down my face
Like asphalt roads through the desert
On a satellite image
My tears are like rivers coiling through a forest
From a bird's eye view
It's like a waterfall falling from my eyes
And it won't stop
I am just so f*cking sad
And I don't even know why

I bend until I snap
And in your f*cking face
You are pushing my limits
I cannot escape you
And I just want some peace and quiet
I want to sort my thoughts
But thinking is impossible next to you
You keep forcing me to accept your ways
Without asking me how I feel
I am not the devil, I just want respect
But you are pushing my buttons
And I really want to punch you in the face
But for the sake of politeness
I ask you to leave me alone
Because it's okay to go our separate ways

When you want to practice
And be perfect right away
It isn't practice
If you don't learn from your mistakes
It isn't practice
If you don't challenge yourself
It isn't practice
And you aren't growing
So, make mistakes and learn
It's okay not to be perfect

When I am overwhelmed
This is what I do
I pick up a pen
And channel the emotion
From my heart
Into my veins
Through my arm
Into my fingers
And into my pen
I leave the words
On the paper
And let my emotions go

I wanted you to be my friend
To support me like a friend would
But you only do behind closed doors
As if you're ashamed to be seen with me
You can't imagine how much that hurts
Because I always support you
Anywhere we are
Maybe it is just your nature
Or maybe it's a conscious decision
Either way, you're not my friend

You have known me all my life
But it feels as if you don't know me
I feel like an irrelevant part of your life
As if you don't care about me
And I want to believe that isn't true
That you do care
But you have given me
So little evidence
That you want me in your life
That I mean something to you
So, I have to accept the harsh truth
And walk away

When you feel like a grotesque failure
In the grand scheme of things
When you feel so devastatingly alone
Know that it will pass
Even when everything looks dark and bleak
Know that the sun will always come out
From behind the clouds
The life will be bright again

Acknowledgements

I am extremely grateful for Butterdragons Publishing, for taking this chance on me and guiding me on this journey. You have made my dreams come true and I will be eternally thankful for that.

I would like to express special gratitude to my English teachers. Mrs. Van Bennekum, thank you for always believing in me. Mr. Waddup, thank you for helping me overcome my eating disorder. I am eating now, sir, I promise. Mr. Paliama, thank you for always being honest with me. In the end, you were always right. The three of you have formed my English. Thank you.

I would also like to thank my bullies. I couldn't have done this without your persistent harassment. I may not have re-written a bestseller, as some of you mockingly said, I have my own book. I may forget, but I will never forgive. Look at me now!

Lastly, I would like to thank my parents, my grandparents, and my best friend. Thank you, for always supporting me, guiding me and believing in me

About Fay van Burg

Fay is a Dutch poet and a fiction writer. She draws her inspiration from heart breaking moments and combines them with her everyday experiences. Her themes of interest are eclectic and vary from online dating to modern views on ancient myths. She writes it all! Fay also uses her voice to draw attention to mental health issues and raise awareness. She writes in hope her words will resonate with her readers and make them feel less alone and believe more in their own magic.

When she's not writing, Fay loves spending time with her lovely horse Shadow and her black cat Salem.

Other BDP books by Fay van Burg

Fighting the Madness
Collection of Tragic Love Stories

www.ingramcontent.com/pod-product-compliance
Lightning Source LLC
La Vergne TN
LVHW090858240726
843527LV00050B/70